the
tears
that
taught
me

MORGAN RICHARD OLIVIER

the tears that taught me

For Cyone

TABLE OF CONTENTS

Introduction

There is a season of life we will all encounter that will stop us in our tracks completely. There will be pain that will shake us to our cores and open our eyes to the facades of life and the truths that stoically stand behind them.

It's a point that we realize it's time to be real with ourselves and our situations. We can't move forward until we dive in and go through it: the pain, pressure, and purpose. This season is painful yet powerful. It is excruciating yet enlightening. It is destructive yet critical for our development.

In order to truly grow and heal, we must understand **the root** of our emotional, spiritual, and personal truth; we must **prune** ourselves of dead mindsets, relationships, and environments to greater align ourselves with peace so that we can intentionally and unapologetically **bloom boldly** into our authentic selves, lessons, and maturity.

There was a time that pain was my only perspective: tear stained pages, ugly truths, and beautiful life lessons. It was the only thing I could see and feel because I was experiencing so many different types of pains seemingly one after the next. From the pain of discomfort, disappointments, and disdain to the pains of loss, grief, and anger: it felt like a never-ending journey of destruction and depression.

My eyes were fully opened, and my heart was shattered. For the first time, I saw the world, my friends, my life, and myself as they were—not as I would have them.

I detached from people I thought I wanted in my life forever, saw my flaws and the issues that came from not correcting them, and began to seek God more than I ever had. I lost loved ones, lost my way, and lost myself. Drained, depressed, and depleted—God picked up my broken pieces and developed my faith, character, and purpose from these very experiences. Insecurities and emotions that were intended to break me built my faith and bolstered my efforts to find myself and a greater purpose.

I cried more in those seasons than I ever had in my entire life. In the same breath, I also acknowledge that I learned more than I cried, as well.

As time passed, self-work ensued and a greater understanding of spiritual warfare, life, and purpose grew. From tears of grief, to tears of growth, to tears of joy—it all began to make sense.

My tears were there to teach me, awaken my spirit, and truly open my eyes. Every single moment was allowed into my life for a reason. Every test God sent me—whether I initially passed or failed—taught me.

My tears were more than proof of my pain. They were a testament of my conviction, pruning, purpose, and impending joy.

To the trials, tests, triumphs and tears that taught me, I acknowledge you. Utilizing the waters the enemy intended to drown me in, God baptized me clean.

the tears that taught me

the
roots

the tears that taught me

With each tear
that crossed my face,
the person I once was
slowly washed away.

If you live long enough, you will experience a pain that changes everything for you. It may cause you to trust less, second-guess more, or fill you with an anger that can't wait to escape.

Whether the pain stems from a person who meant the world to you—someone who has no relevance in your life —or a poor choice of your own, the emotions have a way of sticking around much longer than the experience.

Perhaps the whole point of getting lost is to purposely find your way back to who you are.

It's difficult to find yourself in a season where nothing seems to be going right, and every effort put forward only makes things worse. In every step, there always manages to be ten steps back. Maybe that's the point of it all.

Maybe we are experiencing this level of discomfort because God wants our attention. Maybe He wants us to focus on our mental health and truths within, instead of getting wrapped up in the world and everything around us. Maybe He wants us to experience lack, so we can truly appreciate the growth and abundance that is coming.

Until you lose your peace,
you don't truly embrace and understand
the importance of protecting it.

That's the thing about removing those *rose-colored glasses*. You begin to recognize yourself, your environment, and your life as it is and not as you would have it. It's the beauty of wisdom and discernment that can sometimes feel like a curse.

If you are in a season that seems to be breaking your heart because it's opening your eyes, please know that the pain serves a greater purpose.

For you to grow, thrive, and elevate, you must be able to acknowledge, identify, and understand truth. What you find acceptable will change. How you feel about yourself and other people will change. The environments you want to put yourself in and the conversations you will allow yourself to entertain will change.

That is the point.

You can't walk in spiritual blindness or naivety and expect to reach your destination or place of purpose. With those open eyes—open your mind and heart to what is revealed to you and for you.

Even when you want to believe ignorance is bliss, remember that enlightenment is what will undoubtedly make you better.

Everyone's rock-bottom looks different. What is a minor detour for you can be detrimental for someone else. The same experience that one person may not lose sleep over can be the same experience that sends another person into a downward spiral.

Even good people find themselves
in bad struggles, seasons, and situations.
It is not because they are horrible
but because they are human.

Your mind is a compass.
Wherever your mind goes,
your actions or reactions
will ultimately take you.

My expectations, ignorance, and imagination
have hurt me more than any human ever has.

I've been hurt. We all have.

It's in acknowledging and taking accountability for the pain that I've brought to others throughout my life—both knowingly and unknowingly—that hurt me most. Knowing that my ignorance, insecurity, and issues negatively impacted others not only led me to tears but also led me to search myself and truly change.

the tears that taught me

When you hold yourself to a higher standard,
your lows and losses seem unbearable,
not only because failure and faults
are embarrassing and seemingly uncharted
but also because that feeling of regret and
unwavering shame is foreign to you.

When you break your own heart or fail to practice what you preach, it's different. You not only lose the image you have for yourself but also lose the inner trust that fuels your direction and inner voice.

Sometimes, it's easier for us to pick up shame and sadness than it is for us to carry out rage and reaction. We make excuses for others while holding ourselves to a higher standard all while hiding our pain as they carry no remorse for their part in creating it.

Instead of confronting and exposing those who purposely hurt us, we blame ourselves for allowing them to hurt us. We ignorantly make our empathy the culprit—not their inexcusable acts or intentions —as we unintentionally enable their poor behavior to only thrive and continue.

Whenever I look back on the hardest seasons of my life, I never fail to notice that many of my personal issues began with my inability or unwillingness to address the real emotions at play.

Instead of acknowledging, accepting, and addressing my emotions—I overlooked, overcompensated, or completely overreacted.

It brought chaos to my life and taught me the importance of identifying, expressing, and releasing how I truly felt. Whether if I felt it pertained to myself, people, or situations, I had to be honest and handle the emotions that my heart couldn't harbor anymore. I had to set my emotions free, in a healthy way, so I could move forward.

The truth is, pain will have you trying to control every single detail and person who surrounds your life yet unable to control your own thoughts, feelings, and present.

Anger, bitterness, loss of self, confusion, loneliness, sadness, shame, regret, and insecurity will weigh you down from the inside out.

Search yourself, and be honest with yourself. Don't act off of emotions. Address and release them.

People will either pray for you
or prey on you.

It's your judgment that will determine
if your next steps will lead you to
destruction or development.

Pain has a way of clouding our judgement and leading us to seek forms of healing that only hurt us more in the long run. Sometimes it's the action of us speaking about our struggles that keeps us in them.

We naively outpour our emotions and opinions to the wrong outlets. We so badly want to be heard, understood, or advised that we disclose information to people instead of true wise counsel or the only Power that can truly heal or direct us.

Next time you are in the midst of pain and problems and do not have credible wise counsel in your grasp—remember that you don't have to rush to vent to any person.

Pause, pray, and reflect on God's Word. Seek wisdom. Pursue God's strength instead of another lost person's suggestions.

Don't let your mouth keep you in a cycle that meaningful prayer and counsel can give you the strategy out of.

Stop telling your problems to people
that don't have solutions

Sometimes, we need to
close our mouths
and simply open our eyes.

Sometimes, it's more convenient for someone
to believe or spread a lie about you
than it is for them to accept that
the person who told them the story is a liar.

Your greatest pains and devastations
never come from your enemies.

They come from those you love,
those you'd give anything for, and
those who were blind to the risk
and repercussions of ever hurting you.

the tears that taught me

I placed my confidence
in people's opinions of me
and lost myself
when they changed their minds.

It's easy to say "let it go" whenever the person who's being dragged through the mud, disrespected openly, and side-eyed isn't you.

It's even easier to say "If that was me, I'd tell them off" whenever it isn't your emotions and life involved.

But whenever you feel like no one understands or knows the depth of your issues or truth in a sea of slander, *it is different*.

Whenever you feel like your back is against the wall and you're ready to unleash and push back—don't.

Don't stoop down to any lower level or give an irrelevant person the idea that their words or actions hold any place in your life.

Don't allow lies about you to create lies within you. Be still and know that it may take days, months, or years; we all reap what we sow.

Stand on the truth of who you are and the facts. You don't need revenge. You need to heal.

Dwelling on the fact that people are wrong about you, a conversation, or a situation will not make it right. In life, there will be people who speak on you and judge you without knowing the truth or the depth of your truth. There will be people who openly reject or disrespect you, all while you feel it isn't fair.

No matter what the case may be, you must know that losing sleep, crying your hopes away, or creating a mental prison will not free you from the truth of the matter. The truth is that people will be wrong about you. People will misunderstand you. People will come and go.

Instead of dwelling on the people, problems, and opinions you cannot change— channel that energy into changing your mindset and applying your lessons learned. Use that energy to better understand and love yourself.

You can fool every person who crosses your path,
but God knows your every motive and movement.
He is the one you will never fool
and will always have to answer to.

I prayed that God would remove all in me and my life that didn't align with His plan, and I began to lose everything: my comfort zone, my friends, my mind, and the idea of who I was in this world.

The pain derived from what was revealed and removed brought on a different depression, a type of depression that came from mourning a version of myself that I needed to outgrow because it was out of order.

From there, I began to see that removal as a blessing. He removed my immaturity, my strongholds, and my carnal way of thinking. I lost every thought, person, and belonging I didn't need for my journey.

Learn to handle yourself.
God always handles the people.

It's easy to advise, question, and condemn others
when you have not walked in their shoes,
when the pressure isn't on you,
and when you don't fully know or understand the facts
and factors of their experience.

Some emotions you must experience
to truly understand.

One of the greatest gifts you can give to someone
in pain is the act of listening.

Learn to accept and respect the suffering of others.
Oftentimes, hurt people simply don't want advice.
They need someone who will listen and love them
through their losses and lessons.

A person who will support them through their struggles
without turning them into a conversation piece is a gift.

Whenever you're in the midst of a situation or relationship, your bias and emotions have the tendency to blind you. You are so accustomed to routine that sometimes you fail to see that something is wrong.

For years, I struggled with seeing the bigger picture. I tolerated chaos because I was accustomed to it and found myself drowning in anxiety because I simply couldn't handle it. I didn't even know where to begin.

It wasn't until I detached that I realized what had been eroding my peace for so long. The same practice applied whenever it came to the journey of self-assessment and healing.

I had to distance myself to get a better view of what I didn't want and what I truly needed.

If you are in a season where you are riddled with anxiety, questioning everything, or tired of the trials—I encourage you to take multiple steps back. Embrace isolation, and seek to identify the true impact of your environment and even your thought process.

Giving yourself the space and time to analyze your past and present can very well change the course of your health and future.

When I realized just how much my mindset and words impacted my peace and progress, I began to speak less and work more.

I accepted the truth that it was my unhealthy desire to be praised and supported that left me frustrated and stagnant.

Today and every day, I encourage you to focus on what truly matters. Don't waste time trying to create a life that looks like #goals but you can't stand it.

Don't waste words on people who are hell-bent on hurting you or incapable of receiving the power of your message.

Don't slow yourself down to entertain anything that doesn't bring you peace or align with your purpose.

Your progress is not based on popularity or how many people applaud you. It's based on your energy, alignment, and effort.

Healing has a way of fixing your vision
and feeding your focus.
It's not that everyone and everything
in your life has changed.

It's how you see it
and what you tolerate that has.

There was a time you longed for people to love you.
You prayed that they'd see or hear you. You wished
they could see the depth, truth, and message in front
of them.

Their words, actions, and mindsets pushed you away,
but you always pulled yourself back.

You made excuses like:
"But I love her/him/them"
"But that's family"
"But they've been in my life for so long"

Until you finally told yourself "I can't."

There are some pains, tactics, and revelations you
can't bounce back from or unsee—so you don't. You
just never come back.

To the person that has removed themselves from that
group, friendship, or relationship—trust and believe
that sometimes the right decision doesn't always feel
good and is seldom understood by the masses. Choose
your peace, well-being, and self-love anyway.

Some roads are difficult to leave behind but destructive
to stay on.

Sometimes, we need to take steps back and understand that if we hurt someone, whether knowingly or unknowingly, we have no right to tell that person how they should heal or feel.

The same applies when someone hurts us. Deal, heal, and move forward at your own healthy pace and in your way.

Healing is a process. Don't let anyone manipulate you into thinking you have to progress according to their timeline or in ways that suit their needs.

Everyone struggles.
Everyone fails at something.
Everyone makes mistakes.

Everyone has been the bad guy
in someone else's story.
Everyone has issues
he or she is trying to figure out.

Some people simply do a better job
at hiding those truths than others.

Sometimes, you have to lose the world
to find yourself.

Don't let your discomfort or timetable
lead you to believe that God doesn't have it handled.

He's got it in His way and in His time.
Give everything to Him, and keep it there.

Some battles simply are not ours
to fight or figure out.

Learn to interrupt your negative thoughts.
The more you tell a lie,
the more it sounds like the truth.

Before you let your emotions lead you to act or argue, remember that weak people live for strong reaction. It is your attention that gives them power and your lack of control that will pull you down. Not everyone and everything stand worthy of entertaining. Your words, energy, and time are valuable. Don't waste them.

Some situations are not for you to handle or fight. Furthermore, God will not change some situations if His ultimate goal is to change you. Use discernment, and know when it's time to be still or time to speak. Obedience is what will lead you to overcome.

Some people think that silence reflects an admission of guilt, a person's inability to stand on their own, or a sign of weakness.

Although silence is often misinterpreted, misused, and misunderstood— it is often a power and testament to someone's level of self-control and self-awareness.

Those who know their strength, talent, and worth execute that truth from their energy, actions, or absence. Often, having nothing to say stems from having nothing to prove. When you realize that your words are essentially a form of currency, you quit spending time and effort trying to communicate with those who lack the ability or desire to truly understand.

Going through hard times alone
will show you that you are
much stronger than you think
and can depend on far fewer people
than you know.

Don't pull up a seat with
or vulnerably speak with
those who knowingly eat with
your enemies.

the tears that taught me

When you're at your lowest,
you see who is truly there.

Even if it's just a phone call or a prayer—
your true friends let you know you're not alone.

They are there to convict you and help you get back up.
They love you when you can't love yourself.

Sometimes, the best answer that God can give you is "No" or "Not right now."

I used to think I had it all figured and knew exactly what I wanted in life. In my eyes, I was doing all the right things, knew all the right people, and all I wanted was the idea of more. I needed a better job, better home, and better life. I thought I wanted more money, more clothes, more friends, and more influence until I reached a season that I lacked all peace, all balance, all hope, and all conception of what was happening in my life. My aspirations and prayers went from "God, give this, or I want this" to "God take this from me, or I need you tell me what to do."

I wanted Him to take every pain, bad situation, and emotion away but—like my desires of getting more—He said NO or NOT RIGHT NOW. It later became clear that God wasn't changing things for me because He was trying to change me.

Had He allowed me to keep certain people in my life, I'd still feel out of place and unappreciated. Had He freed me of my struggles and suffering, I wouldn't have the empathy, endurance, or lessons that I have today. I'm grateful for all of the answers of "No" because they aligned me for the many answers of "Yes" and purpose-filled progress.

I was in many people's faces,
but I didn't truly have many people in my corner.
I was a friend to many people
but honestly had few true friends.

That was a very painful and eye-opening lesson to learn
and a truth that I simply can't unsee.

I'm not saying any of those people who come to mind
are bad people—not at all.
The truth of the matter is that they are not my people.

My tolerance levels changed
whenever my mindset did.

There is something about acknowledging
and taking accountability for your own inner toxicity
that leads you to recognize and refuse the toxicity
of those around you.

I refuse to hold on to anything or anyone
that will only hold me back.

I remember seasons of my life where I felt so angry and alone because deep down inside I wanted to do nothing more than go off on someone or on a situation.

I wanted to defend myself, put people in their places, and say what I thought needed to be said. However, that was also a time of my life where I was learning to work on myself, grow spiritually, and walk in obedience. That was a test in itself.

Looking back, I realize that I was learning the power of self-control and the ability to remain calm. I was gaining endurance and empathy from those experiences.

Before lashing out at people, try to learn from them. Even if the lesson is showing that you don't want to be that way or reminding you that silence is a defense mechanism in itself—pass the test.

When people reveal themselves,
believe them.
Stop painting prettier pictures
with the red flags you see.

Some people can't fathom
the idea of growth
because they haven't experienced it
for themselves.

Life is too short
to live it in circles.

Many of us struggle with closure because we lose sight of what it truly is and who's responsible for it.

We prolong our suffering, hold on to screenshots, and replay scenarios in our head, simply waiting for the day to discuss them. We put our healing on hold or begin hating people because we are waiting on them to say two seemingly simple words ... *I'm sorry.*

Here's the thing—that apology may never come. Their remorse may never come. That opportunity to sort things out may never come. At that point, you have to accept the fact that your happiness, health, and how you view your experience from here on out is in your hands.

The moral of the story is that people may hurt you, but it's your responsibility to heal yourself.

Let it go: the pain, the bitterness, and the desire to hurt them back. Stop waiting for them to open their eyes to the error of their ways. They may never see the need to be sorry or the reason to apologize to you. Forgive them anyway. Move forward anyway. Be free anyway.

Close the door to that pain, so you can walk through the doors that are intended, assigned, and aligned for you.

People like to discuss the freedom of healing yet often fail to discuss the feelings and frustrations that come with it.

The truth is, as you grow— mentally, spiritually, and emotionally—you will simultaneously outgrow others.

The toxicity within you will become apparent, and the toxicity around— friendships, environments, and influences —will no longer be ignored.

There may be feelings of loneliness, frustration, and discomfort, but they are not there to merely hurt you. Those feelings are there to get your attention and guide you away from all that is not intended and aligned with you.

Rest assured that all of this is revealed for a greater purpose. Choose to grow, heal, and change.

Evolve even when others don't understand.

Your healing is not found in running off
and creating a new life.
It is created by facing your issues
and returning to your actual self.

MORGAN RICHARD OLIVIER

the tears that taught me

pruning
to
peace

Distance yourself from things
that do not align with your
wellbeing, growth, and serenity
—without the guilt, shame, or fear
of being misunderstood.

There are some prayers where we ask God to remove anything and anyone that is holding us back, and there are some seasons that we live to feel the pain and pressure of those very words.

No matter how hard it gets, how much it hurts, or who understands—we must always remember that God reveals and removes for a greater reason.

There may be some thoughts, emotions, and strongholds that are mentally and spiritually holding you hostage. Acknowledge and address them so that you can heal and move forward with a sound mind, unshakable wisdom, and open heart.

There may be some people who are continually with you but are not truly for you. Seek God's instruction, and discern if they should be moved from their current position in your life or removed completely.

Most importantly, understand that knowingly holding on to burdens and even bitterness can block your blessings.

See past the pain and pressures, so you can soak in what God is truly trying to arrange in your life. Not everyone and everything is meant to, wants to, or is capable of going where He wants to take you.

Put those foolish responses, fake friendships, and fears down. They can't go where you are going.

Accountability changes things.

Remember, if you wouldn't allow it from yourself,
then you shouldn't allow someone to do it to you.

Be patient with yourself whenever your plan isn't unfolding as you thought it would.

Extend love to yourself whenever the world is being cold.

Forgive yourself whenever you fall short or fail.

Give yourself the compassion as you would a stranger, child, or someone you love.

A kind heart is a beautiful thing to share, but don't forget to extend those amazing traits to yourself. You are worthy of your own love and care.

No matter who it is, what is said, or how you may come across
—no one is owed access to you.
No one has power over you.
No one has the place to tell you who you are
or where you should be.

Use discernment, protect your peace, and remember that the only
person you can change or control is you.

You can use many words,
but your actions and patterns
will show me everything.

There comes a point where we have to understand that the door to our lives, love, and future can't be readily open to everyone for various reasons.

Sometimes, it's our forgiving and empathetic nature that leads others to believe that we will always take them back and let them into our lives. Maybe it's the fact that we always looked past problems to keep the peace in our friendships or relationships.

There comes a point that we have to stop choosing people who don't choose us.

If you want to grow, you have to detach from what pulls you down. Free yourself from one sided relationships, wishy wash friends, and those who take you for granted.

You are worth too much to continuously settle for less.

I appreciate and acknowledge the memories we've made. I simply lack the desire and willingness to make more. It's not because I don't love you. It's because I love myself too much to endure or entertain anything and anyone that is not suitable for the person I've become and the person I'm purposed to be.

I had reached a point that I no longer had anything left to say, not only because I knew the best course of action was to be still but also because I had no desire to put myself in the crosshairs of anyone else's ulterior motives.

I was done, drained, and deeply depressed. I couldn't trust people with my pain because I knew that if my vulnerability was manipulated one more time, I wouldn't be able to handle it.

In response, I said nothing while people assumed and said everything.

I allowed my silence and absence to be misinterpreted, not because I feared facing others, but because I feared further losing my mind, my faith, and myself.

I remember the seasons I cried myself to sleep because I thought I was losing people. I was hurt because it seemed like the very people I always tried to keep together were the same ones ripping me apart. That pain, frustration, and pity party went on for quite some time but, eventually, there was a shift.

As time and distance opened between us, so did my eyes.

I began to realize that I gained much more from the "losses" I thought I once had. I gained peace, maturity, perspective, healing, and a greater appreciation for myself and my faith. I gained wisdom and realized that I didn't want a single thing back that I once wallowed in and worried about previously.

I don't care what people will think, how it may appear, or if it's understood. My mental and spiritual health are priorities and worth more than opinions. Without both in alignment, I'm not only at a great disadvantage but also setting myself up for trouble.

You can't put a price on peace, sanity, or balance.

I don't need the extra money if it will cause me to lose my mind. I don't want the friendship if I must sacrifice my growth and wellbeing to stay in the circle. I don't want the job if it will lead me to a place of desolation or depression. I don't want the relationship if it will destroy me from the inside out.

My health and happiness are valuable.
I refuse to waste them.

If bringing up the problems of your past
makes others feel better about the inadequacies
of their present state, then let them.

If people count you out, discredit your capabilities,
or set traps for your demise— then let them.

No human has the power or authority to stop what God has for
you. No human—no matter how much they aim to ruin your
reputation—has the ability to take the content of your character,
the power of your talent, or any knowledge that you've
acquired.

Don't be so focused on who you've been
that you lose sight of all that you're becoming.

I don't hold grudges, but my boundaries remind me that if I don't preserve my peace and order, then I am bound to lose them.

The truth is—as empaths, Christians, and understanding people—we have come to terms with the fact that we are human and are not perfect. We have fallen short, hurt others, and have been hurt. We extend mercy, forgiveness, and empathy because we appreciate that God and others have done the same for us.

However, although we forgive, we must also not forget the truth that not everyone and everything is for us.

Revelation is revelation. Forgive, but know when it's time for someone to be repositioned or even removed from your life. Reconciliation does not always warrant reentry. Discernment is a gift. Distance yourself from fools, or you will become one.

There is a significant difference between encouraging people and enabling them.

I've always had a desire to encourage and help others. I thought if I loved them more, they'd learn to love themselves. If I pushed them more, they'd get the desire to push themselves. I worked so hard to put others together that it eventually started to tear me apart. I had to accept the truth that if others want to change, then they have to make their own changes.

Many people will not change because they do not see the reason to change. Some people don't want to release their strongholds or remove toxicity because it brings them attention.
Others would rather stay stuck because they know everyone else will figure it out for them.

No matter what the situation may be, you can cheer them on, but you can't carry any of their steps or lessons out for them.

You can empathize. You must also place boundaries, so you don't absorb the issues.

If they are still toxic,
you are still unavailable.

There are people who you were always comfortable around that you now can no longer tolerate. It's not because you think you're better or because you look down on them in any way.

It may simply be because those people were compatible with a past version of you but are not suitable for the person that you're growing to become.

Some people have to learn by losing you.

Keep your next move to yourself.
Your enemy can't attack
what they don't know exists.

I'm not shy.
I'm selective.

I don't fear speaking to people.
I simply lack the desire to communicate
with most of them.

You don't hate people.
That's your pain talking.

You love people.

You hate the fact that the genuine strength of your love has been
manipulated, mishandled, or misunderstood in the past which
makes you fearful to love and trust to that extent now.

Don't let someone else's limitations limit you.
You're called for more, and your journey is different.

It's not for them to understand.
It's for you to pursue.

If you feel lonely or misunderstood on your journey
of healing and growth, know this...

Some paths are only yours to take and embrace.
You will lose mindsets, comforts, and people as you grow, but
you will also gain insight, endurance, and a greater appreciation
of your life and yourself in the process. Keep moving forward
and evolving anyway.

No amount of worry or stress
can change or control
what someone else says
or thinks about you.

You will lose people as you begin to gain a greater love of God and yourself. Some will respect your new life and outlook while others will mock and test it.

When you know who you are and whose you are, you will find peace in the fact that you aren't being punished for your faith. You're being pruned and perfected by it.

Now that I've learned and grown,
I find myself more grateful
yet far less impressed.

Here's the truth about growth in any capacity: Not everyone will understand, like, or respect the changes that you are implementing.

There may be environments that you were comfortable in for years that are unbearable for you to rest in now.
There may be conversations you once tolerated which are completely off the table now.
There may be people who you still love today but longer want to be near.

This isn't because you forgot where you began. It's because your mind, body, and spirit are in alignment with where you're going.

All that may have been comfortable and compatible in the past may not be suitable or structured for your future. That is okay. Changing, pruning, and maturing is nowhere near wrong. Honor yourself and your journey by staying loyal to your mental health, personal growth, and spirit.

It's not about the understanding, opinions, or praise of others. It's about the unapologetic acceptance, progress, and peace blooming within yourself.

No matter how much I pray for people
or how badly I want to pull them into my peace,
I find myself fearful.

I'm fearful that if I open my life, love, and loyalty
to them again, they will unknowingly
drag me into their drama
and bring a level of distraction
that I am no longer willing to entertain.

Just as we have the power to choose
which people we want in our lives,
others have that same choice.

Gone are the days that you love people
to the point that you hate circumstances.

Gone are the days that you ignore your needs
to recklessly provide the wants of those around you.

Gone are the days you forget your worth.

No matter who they are, how long they've known you, or who
they claim to be—their placement in your life should never rob
you of your peace, cause you to jeopardize your growth, or lead
you out of self-love.

You can't be everything to everyone else
but nothing to yourself.

My peace increased
as my circle decreased.

When I learned to handle myself and let God handle people, my entire focus, faith, and mindset shifted.

Many revelations broke my heart as they opened my eyes, but I now realize the importance of self-reflection and the harm that comes from reacting out of emotion.

I see just how much more you can control or manage in the long run if you can embrace self-control in times of anger, discomfort, or attack.

I understand that God doesn't bring you through seasons of revelation for you to merely correct others. He sends you, keeps you, and reveals truths to you, so you can correct yourself. He does this, so you can correct the positions you've placed people in your life. In this way, you can work on the issues within yourself.

For many seasons, I was guided and instructed to stay quiet, BUT, in this season, I am here to speak and use the voice that has been developed for this exact time.

In this season, I have no apologies for the joy I am going to experience, no limits to the goals I'm going to achieve, and no shame in the glory that I will give to God through it all.

If you have handled yourself, it's time to handle your business. It's time to make moves that will align you with your purpose and passions. It's time to let go of anyone or any thought that has held you back previously.

It's said that God will make your enemies your footstool; some also prepared you for your platform. It's time to walk in your winning season.

the tears that taught me

I don't need others to repeatedly show me
that they don't value my place in their lives.

There are people who I don't want in my life.
It is not because I hate them or because I'm holding a grudge.
It's because I know better.

Sometimes, we struggle greatly in friendships and relationships because we refuse to accept that a person's season in our lives is over. Other times, we may find ourselves manipulated or feeling obligated to stay in the lives of others who don't deserve us.

Whatever the situation may be, we must understand that what's meant for us will not have to be forced. If love, support, and loyalty aren't reciprocated, then truly ask yourself why you're trying so hard to keep someone around you. You should never have to beg someone to be with you, and you should never be "guilted" into fixing people who only tear you apart.

Check that relationship or friendship's expiration. The people in your life should give you energy—not drain it away.

There is no one on this earth
who I have hatred for,
but there are many people
that I have nothing for.

Cycles continue when we get rid of people,
but we don't get rid of the part of us
that attracted, accepted, or aligned
with those kinds of people.

You can wish them well
and still not wish to have
a relationship or friendship with them.

People who consistently
and consciously hurt you
do not deserve more chances.
They deserve less access.

Detachment does not mean hatred.
It simply means I no longer align with
or allow the energy you bring.

I will let you go before I lose myself.

It's not because I don't love you.
It's not because I don't care.

It's because I know holding on to you
will only hurt me more in the end,
and I no longer allow room for such pain.

I can love you and still release you.

We've grown into and outgrown clothes, mindsets, places, and people. Our bodies have changed over the years. Our goals have evolved, and the avenues we pursue to reach them have evolved as well.

We've changed in different areas, at different times, and in different ways, but we needed all of those changes in order to grow as individuals.

Whether reflecting on a relationship, friendship, or any type of connection—today, I want you to embrace and understand that change is okay. Most importantly, change is needed for anything and anyone to grow.

Understand that truth, give grace as that other person navigates through their journey of growth, and also learn from them along the way.

Encourage each other along your journeys.

There's something uniquely beautiful about looking back, acknowledging change, and seeing the growth of two people (as friends or as a couple) who have pushed through and didn't push away.

I held onto anger, regret, and resentment. I hated those who hurt me knowingly and unknowingly. I refused to forgive myself 100% and others, yet I sat back and wondered why I wasn't mentally or spiritually free.

I replayed failed scenarios, drowned myself in life's *could haves* and *should haves*, and held myself back in many ways.

God has shown me time and time again that He has and continues to work every single thing out for my good. No matter how I feel or what others think, He will show me a way if I let Him.

The very same problems, pains, and pressures that brought suffering turned around to structure me with wisdom, lessons, and a relationship with God that greatly impacted my life.

I say this to remind you that God does not call us to be perfect, but He does call us to walk in purpose.

There are some mindsets, practices, influences, environments and people that you have to let go. There is peace, discernment, and direction you need to obtain.

It's time to silence your inner critic, embrace your journey, and stop concerning yourself with the validation of this world.

Be forgiving, but don't be a fool.

You were hurt,
but you don't hate them.

It only hurts this bad because you love them.
It hurts because you know you never would have
treated them how they have treated you.

We are all capable of failure
yet deserving of forgiveness.
Extend grace and mercy
to yourself and others.

Some people will never know how
much they hurt you.
It's not necessarily because they don't care
but because you never told them.

You can remove someone from your life
and still truly want what's best for them.

Just because there is a distance or detachment,
it doesn't mean that hate has to fill that space.

There are people who made a point to hurt you.

Maybe they lied about you, betrayed your trust, or exhibited behavioral patterns that led you on an emotional rollercoaster for years.

There comes a point that you realize your choice to stay connected or react to such people will only bring you further pain. No matter how bold their efforts were, sometimes you have to quietly let it—and them—go.

There is no need to hold on to a connection that will only continue to hold you back. Let go, and move forward in silence. Keeping your words is not a sign of weakness.

Keeping your peace is your strength.

When the hardest person to forgive is yourself, remember this.

You are human. You are not perfect.
You will make the wrong decisions, experience low points, and even be the bad guy in someone else's story, but that doesn't mean you must be defined by that.

It's time to let *it* go. Whether it's shame, regret, bitterness, embarrassment, memories of failed scenarios, or anger that you hold against yourself—you have to realize that forgiveness of self and acceptance of experiences is needed for you to be free.

If you've learned, repented, changed, and grown since then, there is no need to suffer, condemn, judge, or hinder yourself any longer.

Find the greater purpose of the pain in your past, so you can have peace and wisdom in your present and future. It is time to move forward in forgiveness.

Forgive those people.

There are people who have hurt you knowingly and unknowingly. There are people who you once loved and held in high regard whose actions or words crushed you in a way that shocked you and shifted your focus.

No matter what was thought, said, or done—there comes a point that you realize it's your lack of forgiveness that is keeping you bound.

Forgiveness does not mean that what they did was ever acceptable then or now. Forgiveness does not mean that you will allow that person back into your life or that you ever should.

Forgiveness means that you are releasing the feelings of resentment or bitterness associated with that person or situation. You are no longer allowing it to have power over you. You are moving forward for yourself and not taking the baggage of others or their offenses with you.

Forgive for you.
Pray for them.

It's easier to forgive other people than it is to forgive ourselves because we expect others to hurt us. We know how to release them and pick up the pieces. However, we never expect to hurt others or ourselves in a way than not only destroys our peace but also shatters the trust we've placed within ourselves.

For a very long time, I was the poster child for letting people live rent free in my head. I genuinely gave my last to those who never had intentions of putting me first. I worried about the opinions of others, tried to breathe life into dead relationships, and lost myself trying to find my place in the crowd.

It took a true assessment to see myself and my life as it truly was. Moreover, it made me realize the importance of not only addressing and removing toxic traits within myself but also not accepting or entertaining the toxic traits of others.

Sometimes, you save yourself by removing yourself. It's okay to love others. It's good to extend kindness and empathy. However, whenever the hand you extend has proven to only bring harm to you, it's time to let it go.

Let me tell you a secret. God has a way of making your enemies your footstool.

He has a funny way of using the exact experiences that you thought would destroy you as your foundation for development. Moreover, His way of showing that He is moving in someone's life always seems to go unmatched.

Why? Because God always has the final say—not your enemies, exes, haters, fake friends, or critics. Not even your insecurities have the final say.

Therefore, if God stated and confirmed that something will be done—you might as well calm your nerves, stay in alignment, and keep working because you know it will come to pass.

Get out of your ego and emotions, and remember that no matter how many people are against you, The Winner is on your side.

the tears that taught me

MORGAN RICHARD OLIVIER

bloom
boldly

People will hold on to an image, memory, or version of you that makes them feel stronger, more successful, or better about themselves. Unfortunately, that view of you may be inaccurate, exaggerated, or expired. No matter the case—know that what others think, say, or spread about you holds no weight compared to what God feels, sees, and knows about you. Don't let their opinions become your idol or obstacle. You know who you are and whose you are.

You've been through more than most people
will ever know, and you made it through your
toughest storms alone and misunderstood.

But know that there was a purpose in that pain.
That destruction developed you.
Nothing was wasted.

They will boldly, confidently, and oftentimes falsely scream your shortcomings, rumors, or struggles—yet, somehow, they become mute whenever you're doing well.

It's as if they didn't hear of your accomplishments, promotions, or the strides you've made.

No matter the person or case, remember that weak people do weak things. You don't need their claps, approval, or support to verify your growth, talent, or potential.

Sometimes their silence is validation in itself.

The reason why many people feel stuck
is because they place their identity
in their experiences and insecurities.

You are not your traumas, mistakes, or past.

Though pain has been a part of your story,
it should never dictate your character
or chapters to come.

For the longest time, I thought open doors meant blessings. I thought God's greatest works were seen in things that were new.

In this season, God is making it clear that my greatest blessings stemmed from the doors that He closed. They were doors to things that were old and no longer fit me or the person I was created to become. They were doors that led me to destruction, depression, or distraction.

By closing doors, He opened my eyes and guided me on a walk that led me to wisdom, peace, and purpose.

God is reiterating His truth that every door He closed in my past is connected to every door that will be opened in my future. With Him, I don't wonder about my purpose. I will walk in it, and He will lead me to every door, person, and opportunity to get me where He wants me to go.

I say this to you to remind you that you must choose how to handle your opened and closed doors.

Are you going to worry about doors that have nothing for you behind them or walk through the doors that have been prepared just for you?

As difficult as it may be,
we have to reach a point
where we let go of the burdens
of our experiences and share
the beauty of the lessons
they left behind.

Discomfort is not death.

So many of us are missing out on opportunities and growth because we fear awkwardness or discomfort. It's a part of life. It's time to put that fear behind us. Sometimes, it takes *doing it while scared* to be successful.

For far too long, I allowed pain, irrelevant opinions, and insecurity to push me back in areas where my calling was pulling me.

I held back my words, my truth, and my passions. I slept on my talents, my strengths, and my capabilities.

Make no mistake; I am wide awake and coming for every single thing that is mine.

Not everyone will like, accept, or believe you, and that is okay. As long as you know, address, and embrace your truth—you will grow to understand that another person's opinion of you is not your business.

No matter what you are feeling or facing, know that God is with you every step of the way. Every detour, breakdown, and delay can be used. You are never alone when you are walking with Him.

Even when you feel you are being destroyed, God has a way of using that exact pressure to develop you.

Your thoughts and reactions
have the power to help or hurt you further.

Before acting on emotion, take a step back, and see the bigger
picture. Ask yourself how your response will impact your future
five minutes or even five months from now.

Oh, how I used to go above and beyond to be noticed, appreciated, and validated.

Don't get me wrong, I love to help others. However, in the times of my life whenever I was most insecure, I believed that I needed to make other people happy to be worthy of happiness.

It was my motives, which were out of order, that made me miserable.

As I grew on my self-love journey, I realized just how powerful genuine compassion and charity was for both myself and the other person.

Spreading love, laughter, and lessons without the expectation of anything is mutual healing.

Extend kindness and respond from a place of empathy and not ego.

There is not a single perfect person who walks Earth.

No matter how wonderful they may be, how jealous their social media makes you, or how many people know their name, we are all imperfect humans trying to figure it out for ourselves.

To think of the sleep I lost, the energy I wasted, and the tears I cried because I wanted to be perfect, or truly understood blows my mind.

Learning and accepting this life lesson reminds me to not fear rejection but to live a life that rejects the mediocracy that comes with living a life of insecurity.

We do not need to be perfect or validated by others. We need to be ourselves, learn our lessons, and apply them.

Nothing says "You are irrelevant" quite like taking your energy, time, and attention back.

As long as you're stressed, crying, and concerned—people think they have control over you. Honestly, if you are giving them all of your focus—they do.

There is something powerful about choice.

When you choose to be unbothered, understanding, and unresponsive—those who aspired to shake you are shaken.

Choose to be unavailable to drama, unbothered by pettiness, and unstoppable in everything you do. Quit draining your energy on situations that are only meant to distract you. You have work to do and moves to make.

God allowed people and situations to hurt us.
It is not because He delights in our harm and suffering
but because He knew those pains could lead us
to His purpose and develop our trust in Him.

Not every door that opens for me is sent by God or intended for me to walk through.

Not every opportunity that presents itself is in alignment with God's Plan.

It's having the discernment and obedience to recognize that deep truth that changes so much for us.

I learned this lesson the hard way throughout my life because I once lacked the wisdom and understanding to discern the difference between opportunity and scheme. I lacked the maturity needed to maneuver through this maze that we call life.

Now, I respect and acknowledge the importance of intentional prayer, wise counsel, and strategic planning.

Today, I pray that you are blessed with discernment and clarity to help you make the right decision.

I pray that you make a decision that will come with peace and align you with your purpose, a decision that you've been praying and preparing for. I pray that this decision will align you with your destiny.

Don't rush it. Reflect. Seek your true refuge.

Discover and walk your own path
even if you must do so alone.

As you evolve and embrace all that you are,
you will lose the desire to entertain anyone
or anything that does not align
with your overall good.

I stay to myself.
It's not because I hate people
but because I love my peace.

It took me a long time to understand, accept, and become the person that I am. Please know that I truly do not care if you don't like the woman who stands before you. I unapologetically and wholeheartedly love her.

One day, I want my daughter to look back at my life
and see that I grew from every setback and learned
from every pain, pressure, problem, and promotion.

I want her to understand that it's not possible to be a perfect
woman, but what's important is that she always strives to be a
phenomenal woman.

I am unapologetic about my standards,
unleashing my fullest potential,
and upholding my truth.

I'm unfazed by the enemy's tactics,
unbothered by outside opinions,
and understanding that what's for me
will always be for me.

Knowing and honoring that truth
is not proof of my cockiness.
It is a product of my awareness
and a testament of my faith.

We choose to be bothered
or offended by others.
Most people simply
aren't deserving of that.

Your worth, next move, and confidence
should never lie in someone else's words.
You have power.
Stop giving it to other people.

It's your inner voice that you hear
more than anyone else's.

Water your mind with wisdom
and feed it truths as you focus
on your goals and growth.

I once felt that I needed to answer peoples' questions, tell them my plans, explain myself, or share my wins just so they would know or think I was doing enough.

As I grew, and life lessons could not go ignored, it was revealed that often, I should cover my plans, move in silence, and let my results speak for me.

Here I am—after years of insecurity, confusion, condemnation, fear, and doubt—standing in the confidence that only God could give me and using my talents to open doors that no man can shut.

I'm unapologetically sharing the lessons from my shortcomings, extending empathy to the experiences of others, and pursuing purpose with the passions that bolstered in the midst of my deepest pain. To the person who has been hiding as result of hindsight and holding yourself back due to fear of rejection—it's time to rise.

You've learned your lessons, you've grown, and you're ready to use your endurance and enlightenment for greater things. This is the season where it all makes sense. This is where your energy will say it all, and the comeback will make the setback worth it.

the tears that taught me

I will rise
with or without you.

Go where your energy is reciprocated
not just expected.

Trust me; they are aware.

They just don't want to acknowledge.
They can't understand how everything that
they thought would destroy you
could have somehow been used to develop you.

They can't understand how
all the tactics and schemes
they thought would bruise your reputation
turned around and built your character and credibility.

They don't get it,
and that's exactly why
they don't have it.

They always recognized your potential.
They simply dreaded the day you would too.

Everyone laughs in the beginning.
They mock your efforts,
discredit your development,
and aim to distract you.

Let's see who keeps that energy in the end.

No, your haters don't hate you.
They hate the fact that even after all
of their effort and energy,
you are still growing, still thriving,
and still loved.

the tears that taught me

No one has helped me grow
quite like those who have hurt me.

In their eyes, they are my greatest enemies.
In my eyes, they are my greatest teachers.

It's perspective and embracing the greater purpose
of my pain that brought peace and ignited my fire.

I can't hate them— no matter how much they aimed to hurt
me—because it was their tactics that led me to pursue healing
and spiritual growth, all while teaching me the most.

Some of your greatest blessings
are people who God sent and allowed into your life
to protect you, teach you, and encourage you
along the way.

People that are there to not only love you
but also teach you how to love yourself.

I knew I was happy with my life
when I no longer felt the need to
show, post, or *prove it* to everyone.

We will all experience seasons of pain in life. Whether that pain stems from loss, confusion, failure, or even our own foolishness—we reach a pivotal point where we not only see our true colors but also the true colors of those around us.

We see who genuinely wants to support us in our struggles and who simply wants to see us in them. It is a harsh reality check and wakeup call that is much needed but heartbreaking.

For me, pain exposed my problems and the need to find my place. It also revealed the true position I held in the lives of others as well as the position they should or shouldn't have had in mine.

Time, growth, and acceptance showed me just how much I needed those times, tears, and trials.

I'm grateful for every person who has crossed my path. I no longer dwell on bonds I one time believed I lost because I truly don't want a single one back. I'm simply more appreciative of the true connections that were revealed and remained.

There are no hard feelings—just life lessons.

Then, one day, it clicks.
The pain you had turns into peace as you accept that everything had to happen exactly as it did for you to be exactly who you are now. You hold no blame, bitterness, or resentment toward the experience, person, or yourself. Instead, you see it as the catalyst that led to your change and development. The very storm that shook so much in you also worked to clear your path.

the tears that taught me

What was intended to break you
only built your strength.

I used to question how God could ever turn the worst of my emotions and experiences into something good. I questioned His ability to see me and my life for all that was prophesied when, at the time, I couldn't pinpoint one positive thing about myself.

If I've learned one thing, it's that God sees far beyond our circumstances. He sees how everything will pan out. More than that, He sees our hearts, knows our motives, and never forgets us.

There is always more to our journeys. We simply have to pick ourselves up, get ourselves right, and follow the ordered steps. All things work together whenever we put our pride down and follow the One who knows exactly where we should be going.

Everyone talks about the beauty of growth,
yet the world shies away from discussing
the uncomfortable truth of mourning one's past
self, relationships, routines, and conditions.

No, some things will never be the same,
but *that* is the blessing.

MORGAN RICHARD OLIVIER

Acknowledgments

To the person who has welcomed my words,
I thank you for not only embracing my journey
but also embarking on your own.

I thank you for meeting my experiences with empathy
and accepting my lessons with love.

May you never forget that healing, happiness, and wholeness
are not found by running to the outside world.
They are developed by returning to the stillness within
your most authentic self.

About the Author

Morgan Richard Olivier is an American author, advocate, wife, and speaker.

With a passion for writing that serves as a form of therapy for both herself and her audience, Morgan's outlet for expression fosters and supports conversations that are needed to stop stigmas and support healing, self-acceptance, and personal growth. Since publishing her first book *Questions, Christ, and the Quarter-Life Crisis* in 2020 and her poetry and prose collection *Blooming Bare* in 2021, Morgan has become a source of encouragement and empowerment to men and women worldwide. Through empathy and wisdom from lessons learned, she enlightens and inspires others to find the greater purpose in life's pains and pressures. Morgan's goal is to crush the image and pursuit of perfection by captivating the raw beauty of sincere progress.

INSTAGRAM
@modernmorgan

FACEBOOK
@modernmorgan

TIKTOK
@morganrichardolivier

TWITTER
@themodernmorgan

MORGAN RICHARD OLIVIER

the
tears
that
taught
me

www.morganrichardolivier.com

ISBN: 979-8-9857311-0-1

OAK *Agencies*

Editor: Allister Viator-Martin
Cover Art and Interior Design: Morgan Richard Olivier
Author Photo: Lori Lyman